Dark Octaves

Frank Paino

Longleaf Press

Dark Octaves

Copyright © 2025 Frank Paino

First Edition. Printed in the United States of America.
Library of Congress Catalog Data
ISBN: 9798988762447 (paperback)
Paino, Frank
Dark Octaves: Poems.

Cover Art
Roger Weingarten

Cover Photo
Gerrie Paino "Our Lady of Sorrows" Sculpture by Robert Graham

Book Design
Crystal Simone Smith

....

Longleaf Press

For author inquiries or for information about permission to reproduce
selections from this book contact:

LONGLEAF PRESS
longleafpress.org

~In Memory of Julie Candela

Heard a singer on the radio late last night,
said he's gonna kick the darkness
til it bleeds daylight.

—Bono, "God Part II"

Contents

The Gift of Fire

The Only Kingdom

Late Light

Pietà

The Gift of Fire

Muse

(after Laura Christensen's mixed media piece)

You know
she's not one to speak
unless spoken to,
soothed
by dove coo or tidal tune,
and still
she'll make you work for it
every time,
hip-deep in aquamarine,
lungs tight with held
breath
as the ancient lake closes
over you
smooth as the spine
of a book
that's yet to be opened.
It's up to you
to do the breaking
where gunmetal fish
graze long whiskers
through algal gloom
to read each thing
unseen;
where the twinned weights
of time and water press
the veiled light
of our histories
into a lexicon
for what it means
to be alive
on this ravishing planet
we refuse to stop

breaking.
It will be the new tongue
you speak when,
finally breathless,
you take what you can
carry—
haul yourself back
into light.

Benediction: Whale Fall

On 16 October 2019, the crew of Exploration Vessel Nautilus came upon a whale fall being consumed by deep-sea scavengers in California's Davidson Seamount.

Bless the slick alms
      of your flesh
           pilfered
     by scavenging gulls
          years before
    your last leap skyward.

Bless your unhurried drift
      through liminal zones
           toward the abyssal.

Bless the unlit empire
      that receives you.

Bless scythed rostrum
      forked mandible
           hemal chevrons
      hung beneath
           your broad tail's taper.

Bless baleen.
      Bless blubber.

Bless the castaway beams
      of *Nautilus*
           that render

your bones ghost bright

Bless death's incessant alchemy
       which transmutes
           your stillness
     to clamorous feast
          for octopi
     gape-jawed viperfish
         a shiver
     of bone-eating Osedax.

Bless the fall
       that brought you
          here
     the cage of your heart
         turned to wings.

To the Corpse of Alexander the Great

(Present location unknown)

Whether you lie amidst a tide
      of hymns and tourists' murmurs

that seep past the groans
      of a sinking Venetian basilica

or rapt by the melancholic wails
      that spill from soaring minarets

beneath the city that bears your name,
      we have only scholars to suppose,

though we're told
      with some degree of certainty

your soldiers steeped the abandoned
      house of your flesh in drafts

of wild honey so it would keep
      like a dream of summer

fields on winter's longest day.
      They bestowed on you a second

immortality, beyond
      fame's bloodied crown,

so the hands that raised a sword
       beside them on a hundred battle-

fields might forever grant a sparkling
       commendation, so the lips that kissed

Hephaestion would endure
       through ages beyond counting,

ever full and flushed,
       as with a thousand bee stings.

After Wyeth

(*Christina's World*)

By now I'm certain
you'll beg
for no one.
You aren't crawling
toward a thing—
not the ghost
that cannot choose
between this world
or some other
as it fills, then empties,
the tangled shirt
on its frayed line,
not the bowed ladder
that whispers *run*
as if to spite you,
or the narrow tires
that furrow an old tale
of coming and going.

By now
you're merely weary
of our undiminished gaze,
so you avert
your unknowable
countenance—
you who are fierce
as a prairie flower,
freer than we
who move unhalted

in our heritable grief.
Even the wind
won't let you be,
undoing your hair
like a rumor of fire
that will tongue this field
between us.

Terracotta Army

*The figures in the famous terracotta army of Qin Shi Huang, the first
emperor of China, were painted with brilliant realism; however,
within four minutes of being exposed to air, the pigments fade
completely.*

After more than two millennia,
a stone visage crowns
beneath a farmer's hand.

Soon, a long sleep will begin
to shatter as eight thousand
terracotta men in armor,
horses, acrobats, bronze cranes,
and lazing swans are raised
from their lullaby of earth,
quicksilver, and burnt timber.

But for now, it's just this
guileless man who regards
a long-ago face, fractured
but rendered brilliant
through alchemies of iron
oxide, azurite, and cinnabar
that conjure the artifice of life,

though only for the time
it takes to wonder
at such wild proficiency
before the color flakes,
like scales that sequin
seine nets,

the fragment going dun
as a dried gourd, its hues
not bled but disappeared,
like the dream of immortality.

The Forest

(Freddie Oversteegen 1925–2018)

During World War 1, at the age of 14, Freddie, along with her sister, Truus, joined the Dutch Resistance. She seduced, then executed, a number of Nazi soldiers in the forest near her home.

What is the dim empire of a forest to the Nazi with a Luger at his side
    when a slight girl who straddles the seat of her bike moves her hips
    like the tide's slow arithmetic, cocks her head toward the tree line?

What is it to breach the linked arms of the forest?
    Stilled breeze, twig break, bronze tongue of a distant bell,
        the sun no more than a stutter through the parasol leaves.

How does a wolf lose his way in the forest?
        Lust will drive him through hibernal shadows.
        He will lay down his guard at the mossy base
        of a burled oak, unloose the risen seam of his desire.

How does a wolf die in the forest?
        He will turn his face toward the open mouth of his prey,
        feel her press the blued muzzle to his skull.
        He will hear the hammer fall, learn the way light becomes
        a conflagration, a kiss becomes a requiem.

Candlemas, 1933

(The Papin Sisters)

Now that we've sluiced the blood
from our bodies, put away the hammer

and kitchen knife, set the pewter
vase back on its pedestal,

come lie beside me in these shadows
that gather around the spent glass fuse.

Lea, in another life I was your husband
and you were the girl who drove me to my knees.

How odd is Fate to send me back your sister—
the one who waited seven years for you

to grow round beneath Mother's tattered gown?
Now we've labored that same measure

under this slate and copper roof—
you on your knees before the silk hems

of that simpering brat, your beautiful mouth
stitched with pins and winking needles,

while I stoop over gas jets, stench of sea
bass in my nostrils, and everywhere

polished bells to summon us from each other,
bejeweled fingers stabbing here or there

to spare them from having to speak
so much as a syllable to their mute handmaids,

the two of us supposed to smile as if we might pray
each day to kiss the soles of their sleek

Parisian boots. Tonight, your iron scorched
its silhouette across Mademoiselle's favorite blouse,

and we knew there'd be nothing left
to do but what we had to do. They'd break you

with kicks and the strap that hangs behind
the pantry door, turn us out to savage streets,

the coins we earned locked within their gilded
safe. Lea, let me hold you one more time

inside this narrow bed, nothing between us
but scrubbed flesh. Soon enough the world will

rush in like so much water from a cleaning pail.
Soon enough they'll understand

what we've always known—behind those painted
faces, there was nothing beautiful at all.

The Griffon Vulture's Prayer

A 35,000-year-old flute fashioned from the radial bone of a griffon vulture may be the world's first musical instrument.

After I've lost my place
among clouds,
among muscular
branches,
let the elements
dismantle me
until all that remains
is the slim radius
of one revenant wing
burnished by sun
to brilliance
that will catch the eye
of a woman
clothed in soft hide
who gathers tinder
along a lake's rain-
pitted shore.
Let her lift it
to lips that shape only
some primal tongue,
breathe into
its slender throat
until that solitary note
becomes a melody
returned to sky.

Listen, this world wastes
nothing. Even death
can become a song.

Death's Tailor

(Franz Reichelt, pioneer in parachute technology, 1870–1912)

February in Paris. Zero degrees Celsius
at 8 a.m. & a hard wind freezes spume

like candy floss above the restless Seine.
Twenty pounds of stitched silk cinched with

pale lengths of canvas & two thick,
buckled straps press the vest closer

to his clamoring heart.
The dreaming is over, so too time

for sand-filled dummies
shoved from his third floor

balcony, the music of his sewing machine
a hymn to the suit he now wears—

though savior or shroud is still
one breathless jump from knowing.

And so it has come to this:
three hundred forty-seven stairs

of puddled iron to reach the Eiffel's first
platform where two friends, a cop & a man

with a hand-cranked camera stand
witness as he takes his first unbalanced

step onto a wooden chair,
one more to reach the scarred oak table

from which he will leap into eternity.
Nothing left but forty seconds to lean out

above the ice-rimed earth, wind & whir
of spooled celluloid the only sounds

before he plunges into heedless atmosphere.
There is no way to take it back, no time

for awkward wings to unfurl
before the merciless return to ground

as chill-plump pigeons lift without
care toward the rising rind of sun.

Sarah Bernhardt's Coffin

*The French actress was known to travel with a custom-made pink
coffin she sometimes slept in and in which she famously made love to
the matador Luis Mazzantini.*

It took a matador,
gore still wedged
beneath buffed nails,
to agree with me
the fear of death
is ill-conceived,
waxing crescents
of my hips
pale sentinels beneath
those murderous hands
that clenched my waist
as I straddled him
in the slim width
of that rosewood coffin,
its satin lining pink
as a ballet slipper,
silver fittings ringing
our fevered apogee
as he, at last, delivered
the *volapié*
that rendered me slack-
jawed, eyes fixed
as any martyr's
who beholds
the flung gates
of paradise
but prays her god

for one more draw
of the flay knife,
one more embered arrow
driven to the quick.

Altitude

(Crash of the hot air balloon Zénith, 15 April 1875)

April in Paris. The fields turn
        from green toward rapeseed's gold
                ovation, though such beauty's lost

on these three sons of Icarus
        who keep their eyes on higher things
                as they rise above the cloud line's tumult,

loosing ballast like coins for Charon,
        drifting closer to the cold cathedrals
                of breath's reserved extinction

while the nacelle's give-and-take rocks its measured lullaby
        through *Zénith*'s thermal shudders
                —no matter, no matter—

the slender mouths of oxygen lines
        delirium-missed, unkissed as the lips
                of virgin saints, though here, too, are the holy,

these martyrs of flight and air.
        Two will die smiling
                though their fingers wither to black wicks.

One will fall but live to tell the tale
        of strange ecstasy
                as the barometer's needle dipped—

that secret kept by jealous gods who,
      having lost the gift of fire,
            begrudged the bliss of air.

Rough Alchemy

(Fiji Mermaid—Destroyed in Kimball Museum Fire, Boston, circa 1880)

Hardly a seductress, you were ruined
the moment some cruel dreamer stitched you together

in the creaking bowels of a South Pacific fishing boat,
a thing conjured from savage diminution—one striped mackerel

snatched from its deep cerulean life, scaled back to dorsal fin
and caudal taper, one hapless monkey suddenly missing

everything below her delicate waist. Mermaid. Creature
of sleeplessness, withered breasts that could suckle nothing

but the benthic cold of ocean rifts, who might have dared
to kiss your mouthful of daggered teeth? Still, they paid

by the thousands to stand in the half-light until pupils went wide
enough to summon your twisted form, arms drawn up

as if in wonder, malignant lips stretched in the eternal O
of your rictus. But what was it they wanted to see if not

what they did not want to see? Like the man who staggers
from a bombed-out building beneath the swizzled light of tracers,

eyes fixed on nothing but the place his right hand used to be,
even though he knows it's useless, knows what's left

of those elegant fingers still rests on the Steinway's shattered
keyboard three stories and a sudden world away,

just as his body, in years to come, will refuse
to accept the loss of its song, will trace a spectral twin

under Kirlian light sapphire as Chernobyl's half-life
until he comes to believe that insistent, luminous print

is a small voice crying out from a ruined city,
the wild prophet of a promised reunion that waits somewhere

beyond his terminal breath. And who among us could refuse
such rough alchemy, a world beyond what merely seems:

mortar rounds breaking twenty-seven bones against eighty-eight
wooden keys, but only for so long. Or you, misshapen offspring

of ocean and earth, rising from the inferno's crucible, no longer
monstrous, but something beautiful. Something bright.

Lot's Wife

Of course you knew your options,
grasped the admonition spat like hot coals

from the angel's snarled lips.
You knew you held the power

to resist that resolute turn
toward the scorched horizon

of everything you treasured,
to keep, instead, the council

that proclaimed a wife's salvation
is secured in her husband's shadow.

You couldn't say you were never
warned, weren't granted a second chance

for clemency the moment you considered
dereliction—blood-warm tide singeing

your throat like Dead Sea water,
sinews cracking like quail bones

against a lost tribe's molars.
You knew love was its own conflagration,

knew sand that boiled
between your toes as you spun

was kindred to the glittering fate
that would transmute you to nothing

more than a cautionary tale. Still
you turned. Woman of salt

and cinder. Woman not even conceded
the simple blessing of a name.

Or else it is mine. Is everyone's.
Is the jagged sound of our breath

in the moment we must choose
to face the fire or flee.

Thích Quảng Đức

First, a baptism
        of gasoline
that translated saffron
        to deeper gold,
then, a mirage's
        shivering vapor,
the Austin Westminster's
        cool blue hood
forever frozen agape
        as if in silent witness
to the impassive man
        who struck
a match as casually
        as an offered light,
as if to steal Death's thunder,
        as if to say, *No*
matter how close
        you hold me,
I will hold you
        closer still.

First Law of Thermodynamics

For we are the wolf,
and we run with its fathomless
hunger. We inhabit the elk
that is its prey. For we spark
in rain's silver, the glint of sun
on snow. For we are the stone
borne to sea by a fleet river,
and we are the river. For we
shall become sand that was
stone. For we are ghosts
comprised of nothing
but the breadth between fire
and fire. For what burns is
dismantled like the scent of
woodbine unpetalled
by breeze. For we are stars,
and the stars' last light.

Topsy

Elephant electrocuted at Coney Island, NY
4 January 1903, 2:45 p.m.

No matter the years without mercy,
brash men with their bullhooks,
a pitchfork perforating the gorgeous curve
of jaw that mirrored your absent tusk
line, sand in your eyes from children
delirious with cotton candy
and their brief autonomy, your trunk tip
singed by a drunken handler's cigarette.

No matter the years of chain chafe, train jostle,
and the raucous cries of ticket holders
hell-bent on getting their money's worth.

It all came down to that ten-second
intermission between breath and
stillness—too brief for human ecstasy,
too long for lightning to sear
your body's wet pathways—
6,600 volts carried nine blocks
from Edison's substation
into Luna Park where you'd refused
the bribe of apples meant to charm you
across the timber bridge to that spot
beneath the rising electric tower
where spectators shuffled
from foot to foot to keep warm
through the hours-long waiting.

No matter your immovable frame.
They simply rerouted death
to meet you, cables coaxed
twelve extra yards to where you'd halted,
carrots laced with cyanide
unable to tamp the mounting panic
as harsh men strove to tether you.

And though the grainy film stutters
in shades of ash and charcoal,
who can fail to see the citrine sparks
burst like infernal blossoms
from the copper fittings
you'd tried to shake from the great spades
of your feet, pale smoke snaking
the coarse columns of stiffened legs,
your spine's jittery arc
fingering the clotted-cream sky—
a few more wrinkles in the hem
of a gathering midseason storm.

The Only Kingdom

Lucifer, Falling

To be suffered

spirit into matter

to be unloosed
from perfection's tedium
into the wind's shrill
hammers

into gravity's harsh tug

to be made flesh

suddenly struck
match-bright
with desire

the gift
of your sweet
diminishment

Apocrypha: The Ram Considers Abraham

And what if *my* god demanded of me
     blood

of my own kin, a ewe, still unsteady
     on spindled legs,

for an offering? What if I led her
     to pasture, to the hackled wolf

hunkered amid the tall grass?
     What if I turned

only when the screaming
     wind became an angel's

tongue calling back the Lord's
     command like a man who swallows

hemlock and lives
     to tell? What if, in praise of

that late mercy,
     I guided the wolf to the tent

where your firstborn slept
     unattended, tangled in dreams

sweet as the psalm buried
     in his mother's breast?

Blue

(after the 40 Martyrs of Sebaste)

All night they have drifted
just beyond the lake's blue lip,
forty men, once soldiers,
now little more than an iris of ice.

Sometimes, a thin voice rises
in a jittery psalm,
though mostly it's the bone chatter
of yellowed teeth coming together
like snapped tinder that signals
the women who kneel
on the frozen mud
their sons have not yet opened
the door to perpetual light.

Each man has turned away from
the bonfire that beckons on shore,
white at its heart like the breath
of horses that tug at the stub grass.
Each man has renounced the bath
whose steam turns the air to crepe.
Each, except one who, near dawn, surrenders
his resolve to the waiting arms of his captors,
though the sudden heat of that blue seduction
stills his heart mid-beat in its blood sac.

For a few moments they float,
tilted as a table with one leg broken,
until one of the guards sees the bruised fist
of sky rain forty crowns of scintillant ice,

immerses himself in this new conviction,
and they are forty again, suspended
in mirrored sky blue as rain, as unopened veins.

Near noon, they dream their limbs
grow warm. Toes first, then calves,
muscled thighs. A bone ladder
to reach the cooling heart.
Each man in turn drops
his jaw at the pleasure. The taste
on their tongues is the taste of women
they have known. They die together,
like a wish exhaled over candles.
Here was light. Now nothing
but a blue seam to seal the sigh
of each final ripple, each upturned face
that lapped at the gate of paradise.

Magdalene

Because she is in love with his lack of desire,
        the way he takes her hand as one alike,

she brings perfume desire paid for,
        pours it like an extravagance of tears

that carve a finger's trace
        through the dust beneath his ragged hem

till it wastes like oil from a shattered lamp,
        like the blood bloom that will burst

from the wound of an iron spike
        driven hard through the slope

of his olive ankle
        toward which she presently declines,

hair sable as moonless sky,
        long enough to be both rein

and veil with which to blot contrition,
        his name untangling from her tongue

like a favorite song.
        Later, when he is chill white

as an alabaster jar and broken
        in the womb of a cleft mountain,

she will touch him once again, soothe
    what the world has wearied in him.

Nesyamun

*(Priest and scribe of the Karnak Temple whose mummified remains
are displayed in Leeds City Museum, England)*

Forty layers
      of incensed linen
stripped
      in the slow
seduction
      of science.

Cumin, myrrh,
      oils of cedar
and cinnamon
      whose aromatics
swirl
      like the potent scent
of burnt
      offerings.

Here, beneath
      a layer of spice
and sawdust,
      your face
relinquishes
      perpetual dark.

After three millennia,
      your mouth
bares
      teeth dazzling as
minnows
      in an evening

lake,
        soft palate
fallen
        like the roof
of an abandoned
        temple.

We're told
        it may have been
a honeybee,
        all swift hum
and needle,
        who stung
your song
        to stone.

Filia Luminis

(Virgin & Martyr)

Begin by choosing a name—
something round as a pebble
beneath the tongue:
Theodora. Philomena.

Now place her, robed only in her
extravagant locks,
before an amorous emperor
whose desire she rebukes
in favor of an unkempt man
with sunlight glinting through
the open bones of his wrists.

She will say *no* to the jewels
she's offered, overstuffed coffers
of silk, silver platters of glistening
fowl and plump olives, though,
most of all, the tumescence
he seeks to hide
beneath his ringed and braceleted fist,
so he will lay her on the smoldering
bones of the faithful,
though she will only sigh
like a young wife
in the arms of her beloved,
refuse to join
the heavenward sweep
of cinders. To die only once
for love could never be enough.

From here, your story might turn
to the unblemished slopes
of her shoulders, lily throat bared
to the blade that will glance
off bone, leaving the jugular
whole, her voice a wet wind
in the gape. Or a glowing brand might
singe the undefiled vault of her womb,
though even then she will not cry
out, being wholly absorbed
with the radiance that encircles her heart
like a crown.

In a matter of days, something no more
or less brutish than what went before
will finish all her refusal began.

Gather her remains. Cast them
in a swollen aqueduct
from which she might rise
in the form of a dove
that wings its way
toward the eastern horizon.

If not, there's a little more to tell.

The water must become
miraculous and she, ubiquitous,
poured from earthen pitchers
or warmed in steam baths
where slaves scrape oil
from the backs of their captors.

Saints and sinners will swallow
her, float over the fractured cusps
of her teeth. The withered arm
will be made whole.
The stillborn child will suckle.
Holy water. Holy ghost.
The virgin both entered and entering.

Judas: Triptych

Rabboni, I did not fail
to notice the way your hair shone
with the gloss of that harlot's fawning,
your brow and calloused feet gone slick
with oil and kisses, her robes sapphire
as summer skies against the slender throat
of alabaster from which she poured
the spikenard, its musk ghosted
with a rumor of something long hidden
among a crown of roots and relics.
What wouldn't I have done to take her
place beside the tattered leather
of your sandals?

Remember. I did only what you said
was ordained before the first blades
of starlight were fashioned to shatter
unbroken space. Tonight, I turned
from your talk of bread and wine, fled
beneath a sickle of moon brilliant
as a purse of silver, slouched
where Gethsemane's trees trembled
in hot breeze, until your slender silhouette
fell across the footpath. I swear,
all the world caught its breath.
Then the taste of your mouth—
hyssop, olives, bitter hint of sow thistle.

Confess it. Without me, you would have
lingered those lightless hours in the garden,
fear-fevered, damp with sweat and blood,

but unmolested. I did only what was dreamt
into your story. Even so, I grant, again,
my *fiat*. Let me be the scapegoat,
cast out and cursed down the ages.
Let my ruin be delivered
through burn of rope or bowels spilled
across a patch of midnight field,
only do not turn your face from me,
My Lord. You, who are the only kingdom
into which I ever longed to enter.

Lazarus

Truth be told, from where he stood,
there was simply *now* and then

what none of us can say with certitude,
though we may have no doubt

about the ragged lullabies of women
wailing, the notes of myrrh

stitched between aloe's succulence,
the dazzling linen chrysalis

in the shape of the man within,
who either hung between two worlds

or none
as they laid him in the hewn rock cleft

and the indifferent weight
of the mountain settled around him.

About the rest, it's up to each
to believe or not, that within

a rough palm of stone
the white flame of a corpse

stirred to a distant voice crying out
like a son for his father

gone before him into war—
whether it was the man who lifted his voice

or the one who heeded his call
that winced against the dumbstruck light.

Afterward: Magdalene

According to legend, after the death of Jesus, Mary Magdalene fled to Provence, spending the remaining 30 years of her life in a mountain cave where, daily, angels transported her to heaven as a foretaste of eternity.

To kneel in the slick
palm of a cave
each morning,
its walls scintillant
with torch
and candleflame.

To clothe yourself
in nothing
but the extravagance
of your sable hair.

To step into
the ascendant
light above a valley
where hooves of bulls
and wild horses
churn the marsh
water to froth.

To have eyes
no longer in love
with earth but only air
that murmurs
at your approach

like a host
of honeybees.

To be the cynosure
of angels
whose breezy hands
encircle your wrists
like spindrift
as they lift you
past the white
mountain.

To be hymned
one solitary hour
each day
and not a heartbeat
longer lest you die
of ecstasy.

To be a woman
once fallen
into the beds
of wanton men,
into the open jaw
of a chiseled tomb.

To be the one
who rises now
like the exquisite
seduction
of a costly perfume.

Rapture

after the last unyoked plane
has dragged its terrible plume beyond
the horizon and the last car
its wheel unhanded
has coasted to standstill or twisted
its frame to a wreath of steel

after the last father has tossed
a laughing son or daughter skyward
and been left empty-handed
on the downside

after the last note of the last hymn
has sung itself into infinity
beneath the arched and worn doors
of worship's still houses
and the sky's grievous wound
has been stitched
like mouths of the dead

those of us who had nothing to pray for
nor hunger for taking leave
will bend to gather our strange harvest
vacant hoops of wedding bands
creased pants and cheerful dresses
left in heaps where they hollowed

the days will still go from gold to gold
the magnolia will shed its pink and cream
in the uptick breeze
the sparrows will scavenge thread
from torn armchairs in desolate rooms
whose curtains will frazzle
in the windows' perpetual gape

at dusk we'll lie down to regard
the luminous breadth of the stars
which has always been plenty
which has always been more than enough

A Kind of Benediction

(St. Isaac's Cathedral, St. Petersburg, Russia, constructed
1818–1858)

And who could blame them if they found in their falling a
kind of benediction, like the sleep that descended swift as a
scimitar each dusk they slouched home to a hurried repast, a
hurried moment inside a woman who would one day tell a
son or daughter how their father's hands fashioned the
shimmering crown of Saint Isaac's, though the truth was little
more than serfdom—forty years of sixteen-hour days
bent to gold amalgam and smoldering mercury to make the
walls and arches, the towering length of the grand iconostasis,
glitter like the streets of paradise.

How many cups of liquid silver did they burn to make each
halo shine? How many rungs on how many ladders to ascend
the scaffolds for a few rubles and the glory of their hidden
god? How many years before sixty men felt sweat soak their
flesh despite ice that clung to their beards, before blood-tinged
foam closed their throats as vertigo turned the world on its
shimmering axis so they tumbled from the dove-capped dome
like stars no one would dare to wish upon? And who could
blame them if they found in that falling a kind of benediction
from a god whose hands, if suddenly unloosed, would surely
have written above the poisoned cupola his mortified errata.

Saint Fillan

Saint Fillan is said to have had a luminous left arm that allowed him to read and copy his Bible in the dim light of the cave in which he dwelt.

I came to scour the hollow inside me
where desire cradles its sour heart.

I have shrugged off the rough serge
of my habit, walked bare-skinned
through bull thistle and blackberry canes
to flay the demon of each coarse longing.

Here, where vesper light speaks of
heaven's lost horizon, I have plunged
my recalcitrant flesh
through the river's scrim of ice.

I have singed with salt these lips
that ached to kiss a woman's breasts,
thrust into the hornet's paper
lantern these hands that sought
to trace a silken back's slight camber.

For what is the body if not a curse
that must be broken?
Come flail. Come spiked cilice.
Come thirst and maddest hunger
that renders each bone dry as tinder.

And for recompence, my Lord,
you have granted the torch glow

of my own slow burning
which tongues radius and ulna
to a hundred candle's brilliance
that I might unbind the meaning
of Your holy word,

as in another life
I might have lit a nuptial lamp
before undoing the soft laces
on my bride's pale wedding dress.

The Whale

I never asked for this,
never wished to be the vessel
of gloomy prophecy,
nor could I grasp the mathematics
of your eased consciences
summed to skins of ash
beneath the graze of sackcloth.

I breached my way into your myth
through the simple arithmetic
of bad timing,
arrowing the crepuscular sea
toward a thumbnail of moonglow,
lungs filling like storm sails
just as the old man was tossed
from the stern's scarred gunwales,
past baleen and pink skim of tongue,
then caught like a cherry pit
in the throat of a gasping child
until I spat him back into the tidal tug
of Nineveh's wakeful shore.

To me he was nothing
more than a bellyache. I found no use
for him or the ways of men,
your high priests wailing in temples

whose polished lanterns would someday spill
the light of all that once sustained me
in my guiltless solitude.

The Beloved Disciple

Lord, let me rest my head
above the prison
of your heart,
its blood psalm swift
as winnowed flames
that clear a field
for someday's harvest.
Let my own heart sing
in faultless synchrony
and so be hidden
in the selfsame song.
Let me take
the Magdalene's place
at your feet,
caress the bones
that will be shattered
like tablets of stone.
Let me place my hands
upon these wrists
that will lift you
to each staggered breath
in the failing
pre-Sabbath light.
Master, let me
press my mouth
to the tender space
between your ribs
that will be opened
like a sepulcher
that cradles nothing
but a hollowed

winding sheet,
as if the man
once laid there
walked out
into the garden,
unclothed
and unashamed.

Saint Giles's Doe

*Saint Giles, a French hermit who lived in a forest cave, survived
solely on the milk of a deer that came to him for this purpose. One
day, hunters pursuing the deer accidentally shot Giles with an arrow.
As a form of penance, the saint refused treatment and was left
disabled for the remainder of his life.*

Sometimes she comes bearing the scent of sun, wild
meadows. Sometimes snow mantles her back

like a scattering of ash. Sometimes, as the story goes,
the hunter's arrow sings past her like serendipity's mad

fortune, then on through the royal forest's dappled light
to find its mark in the saint's right femur or the beggar's bowl

of his belly, else it splinters the delicate frame of the hand
raised to save her. No telling and no matter but the lesson

of his elected negligence, which leaves him halt
and haunted by the penitential throes of that sharp legacy.

On a single point each history agrees:
he was sustained by a doe whose milk proclaimed

a foretaste of eternity—persimmon and cool brook
water, beechnut, hickory, and September's dusky

merlots. Nights, his hagiographers record, Giles laid aside
his rosary and worn psalter, knelt before her velvet

underbelly and gave praise, his mouth become a bell
whose silence was its only song.

Lazarus's Wife

On the fourth day, he returned
to me, breath fetid

as the smoke plumes of Gehenna,
eyes empty as a graven effigy's.

Now, flies nimbus the plates
I leave for him outside

the shadowed room
in which he shelters.

Still, he quaffs wine,
delights in how it streams

in bloodred rivulets
through the welter of his beard;

and whether I kiss or
curse him, his tongue is still as

an unblemished dove
charred upon the High Priest's altar.

Evenings, he steals across
the cool floor of our bedchamber.

When he enters me, it is as if
each thrust is meant to outpace

some dread shade that gains on him.
Mornings, I wake to blades

of sun where last he laid,
a leaden ache like hurled

stones between my breasts.
O, I rue the Kriah, my face

pressed to dust
in supplication. I rue the one

who came in answer, stood before
the sepulcher and summoned.

Daphne, Again

(for my mother)

After the fire
after the simple division
of flesh from bone
bone from ash
we took what remained of you
poured it like mercy
beneath the weeping katsura
while crows wheeled
beaks stained
with plundered berries
and the monuments behind us
crouched
heavy with old griefs

Once
not far from that place
the city's river burned
like a requiem for the old gods
but today
men tend the ore boats
flick their cigarettes
across the water's surface
with brusque impunity

Mother
I no longer believe anything
to be impossible
I have seen a river
put on a cloak of flame
I have seen you turn from flesh

to something unyielding
as stone
from cinder to ash
the worms will turn
to leaf the tree

Late Light

Anorexia Mirabilis: Catherine of Siena

Boy-boned Catherine, barely a curve
from clavicle to cleft, you taught me
blood's no necessary instrument. Some
martyrs die by increment: tang of a
brined green olive, wet cusp of sun torn
sweet from the rind—each bite you
took obliged its own unkind
annulment—grey shaft of a goose
feather to score the sensitive damp at
the back of your throat or, sometimes,
the chartreuse pester of fennel fronds;
every act of loathing your woman's
form transmuted to a strange hosanna,
a sanctus bell that beckoned your
heavenly groom to part the wound in
his side, let you lap at the blood and
water, your mouth a brief ciborium.
Catherine, patron saint of forced
emesis, of young girls with newly risen
bones, your greatest fault was to covet
a heart bereft of all desire save what he
asked in each strike of nail through
wrist and ankle, that tenderest spot
beneath your right breast, five flames
descending from the cypress cross, five
opened gates that drove you back from
the worn communion rail, ghost-
branded, wedded to thorn and scarlet
cincture, swallowing no more for the
rest of your days but the accidents of
flesh in wafer, wine's open-veined
intinction, though even when you were

finally spent, a hollowed effigy in cream and ash, adrift in a lily-thick coffin, your confessor judged you not yet small enough to drift through the eye of heaven's needle, and so he parsed you like some demon's dowry: left foot to a Venetian bishop's summer home, wan smile of rib above a Florentine high altar, and, under glass, for the faithful back home, your white-veiled head, afloat in the candle's antumbra.

Fiat to Autumn

to the sun that daily casts its requiem nets
          of twilight
                    sooner
across the coppering meadows

to the phoenix forests
that candle each branch without flame

to the brown bear who plunders
          briar bramble bin
                    the scavenged silver streams

to the dog who fish flops
          in the jazzy leaves

to the frost that shivers
          the mare's luxurious muzzle

to the psalter of birds
          who tilt their wings
                    toward warmer latitudes

to the ghosts of vanished things
          and to the ghosts themselves

Fiat
to my heart that reckons
          its own measured season

to my flesh that will one day ascend
    —here smoke here cinder—

   toward the loom stars
      from which it was woven

Hellebore: Lenten Rose

I ask nothing but winter's white
antiphon, earth's breath caught
until the sun's reeled back
from its distant hemisphere.

My face I keep turned
toward the unhurried undoing
of fallen trees, of gore spilled
from the buck who, too late,
startled at the staccato snap
of twig break.

Call me darkness visible,
call me kin to belladonna
and mandrake,
I, who was conscripted
to poison the wells
of walled cities, to still
the sanguine tides
of Alexander's thundering heart.
I, whose toothy leaves greened
a balm to whirl wise women
around mad Sabbat flames.

Come now, lift my gaze
from its dim ruminations.
Behold sepal, stigma, nectary.
Kiss me, if you dare,
parse and consume me
like the lust of forest floors.

I might waste you in this half-light.
I might grant the gift of flight.

Dead Hummingbird

And the great earth, with neither grief nor malice,
Receives the tiny burden of her death.
                              —A. D. Hope

She rests roadside, nearly under the graze
of my sandal, small as an infant's hand cupped

to catch a palmful of air, casual as a foil wrapper
tossed from a car window, no sign of what pulled

the sky from under her. The once-delirious blur
of wings, more insect than avian in their hectic buzz

and whir, lay unmoved by fragrant breeze. Sealed, too,
like parchment and wax emblem, her elegant beak

so often thrust into vermillion throats of trumpet flowers,
their sweet tongue-kiss of nectar. Stilled, yet not unstirred,

her breast rises with its freight of pale guests that writhe
and coil where once her frantic heart glistened,

though soon enough will come the alchemy of flesh
transmuted to a thousand-thousand wings that will lift,

then scatter, however brutish in their flight.

For a Couple Who Died Two Days Apart

Winter's no season to vouchsafe hearts
but these two made do with even exchange,

bone white for bone white, quiet as a forest
through which some unfamiliar beast

has lately passed. Underfoot, they lie here,
one atop the other as, breathless in life,

they may have traded places
against the tousled sheets—slack-jawed

and joyfully astride—windows ajar
in equal measure to spring's fecund chorus

or autumn's flaming elegy. Winter for now or
forever: no matter to these lovers wedded beneath

hoarfrost and hunger, their contented erasure
like staves of music that molder on a forgotten page

until their vanishing itself becomes the song.

Evening Wind

(after Edward Hopper)

Day burns its wick
to gilt horizon:
behind the still damp
washbowl,
the room gathers
shadows like an apronful
of obsidian
as she bends a knee
to raise herself
onto the rumpled
bedsheets, quiet
in that moment
between work and ease,
flesh suddenly
expectant
as sheers lift
in the unseen—
white and white
like winding sheets
unfurled in the cold
mouth of a chiseled tomb—
but first the susurrant
seduction, the dizzying
breath of praise.

Nocturne for an Unidentified Girl Found Murdered in a Field

Where a girl whose name we might never learn
    who could not have been more than thirteen
    teeth white as a furnace core
    smiled
    for the camera
        how the sun ticked low
    for the man who fingered
        the shutter button
            in languid quarter moons

Where the sky was shrouded
    by the shape of the man
        astride the girl
            who was no longer
            smiling

Where crows rose like an omen
    too late
        for its own grim heeding

Where the summer field
    became a shroud
        a dirge dragged through coreopsis
    while the world turned on its cold axis

For the Dove at the End of This World

This time, she'll be loosed
from a fortress adrift
in a sea of withered earth.
She will not return
with an olive song
cinched in her beak,
only a snarl of fishing line
and hypodermic
silver that ghosts the rise
of each beaten wing.
There will be no next
time, only an ashen
bird who finds no asylum
where the world arcs
at its horizon,
her feathers aflame
in this late and failing light.

Faith

From 1906 to 1912, bell diver William Walker spent six hours, six days per week, shoring flooded wells beneath the sinking hulk of Winchester Cathedral to make possible the reinforcement of the building's crumbling foundation.

To know the mortised weight of the cathedral,
      its ancient back breaking, hangs

above him like a kingdom that will surely fall,
      and still to seal the brass bell

against water's breathless intent,
      to be tethered and dropped

past twenty feet of chalky marl and peat,
      sunken medieval timbers that groan

like the damned in their infernal dungeons.
      To see nothing before or behind

so each searching finger
      becomes his only salvation:

here the lax underbelly that means to
      swallow a hundred graven saints,

here the rope that leads to the ladder
      that leads to the light.

To suffer six years of this measured
      rising, rung by weary rung.

To keep his solitary watch,
       restraining unwearied tide, bending

his back to the insufferable *next*
       and *next*, each pallid sack of concrete

a paschal flame snuffed
       as the flood pool closes around it.

Even then, to carry on through the fallen black.

Still

Late October, and the painted turtle
who, summer days, staked her claim
on the upthrust fist of an old pier piling,
lifts her head for a final portion
of sun before she drops her body's plated
anchor into the cooling lake—past jade
combs of eelgrass and milfoil, snarls of
hornwort and fishing line, to the place
lily pads purl their roots.

There, she hollows the soft tomb
in which she'll lie till spring,
armored scutes like amulets with no light
to set them burning, while Canadian winds
dive into Ohio's northern counties, seal
this small lake with a pall of tarnished ice.

Eyes closed, limbs drawn into their cage
of keratin and bone, she'll go still
as a saint who contemplates heaven's
lanterned footpaths, heart gone quiet
as the tongue of an untolled bell,
life hinged upon that last in-breath
while lactic acid pours its poison
spell into her veins and her body
begins to surrender its only antidote,
leeching calcium from bone and shell until
she begins to soften, the weight of water

growing in equal measure to her piecemeal
vanishing, the cure nearly worse than
the curse, nothing to sustain her but this
fraught tranquility that will vouchsafe the days
lengthening toward April's green ubiquity,
that fist of softened pine which will hold her,
once again, in summer's scintillant thrall.

Upon Being Buried with My Twin

And so we'll find ourselves some *one day*
together in earth's primordial clasp,

perpetual night enfolding us
in its rich gesture of comfort,

the beat of distant freight trains
like the synchronized pulse

of spent lovers, the two of us silent
in this new womb,

your white shroud candling
the pitch, my velvet bag

of bone and ash pressed
above your heart,

patient for time and elements
to undo the seams, sift me

between the wax and wane
of your crumbling ribs

like sand in the throat
of an hourglass as we await

our measured resurrection
through roots of beech,

through bole and branch
into leaf, into summer's chartreuse

and silver, autumn's slit wrist
red and umber.

Winters, we'll rattle like dice
in a gambler's palm,

fracture horizon like lightning
against wild and ravenous skies.

What Light Is Given

The boatman tells me eyeshine that spangles
these high-summer shallows comes from gators

that dangle their primeval bodies like lightning
rods fixed between two atmospheres, their heads'

blunt shovels barely clearing the lake's static face,
armored tails wicking the cool six feet under toward

equilibrium. Even if it's not true, I believe
in the stolen light of their eyes beneath a scythe

of moonfall, the vertical bruise of their still forms hung
like pendants of polished jasper. Even if it's not true,

I believe their stony patience for whatever my skiff might
hold will be surrendered in favor of the leaf-rich bottom,

its blanket of slick decay like a cold fever rag. If I'm wrong,
this dun water might roil like silver underbellies of leaves

in storm, my destiny death-rolled in a mouthful of
daggered teeth. And if there is another life, will I wake

to some new heaviness I'll carry as on earth I did
desire? Or will I simply drift like these ancient predators

who've learned to abide diminishment, to take
what light is given and make of it some brighter thing?

Winter Solstice

Day bleeds out too soon
      in this frozen hemisphere.
Midafternoon. Already,
      ice throws back
the flicker of stars'
      lesser light,
night gathers
      its smoky hem, rises
for its longest revelry.
      Concealed in holly
hedge, a winter bird stirs,
      shakes free a hail
of wizened drupes
      faint as an old blood trail.
In this sudden dusk,
      I can do nothing
but name all that burns
      of its own accord:
arterial gush of flame,
      willow, witches' butter,
hellebore, each promise I can keep
      in whatever time remains.

The Harrowing of Hell

The dead have learned
to make peace
here, to glide
in the sleepy eye
of the tempest,
lantern stars
only a somnolent myth,
the dark no longer
wordless but a song,
a mother cradle
for their aimless rocking,
their occasional, sweet
friction, every touch
a ravishing
spark
in the borderless
gloom.

Now
he stands here,
raining light
from his wounds,
right hand poised
to fracture
this perfected
equilibrium
where each has turned
from the tattered
flags of trespass,
has already blessed
or absolved the other

for what lies
buried
in the world
that forsook them.
Not one will reach
to caress
the fragranced hem
of his winding sheet,
nor pant after
the starry path
that wakes him.
There is no kingdom
more comely
than what they have
wrought
out of their nothingness.

Where There's Smoke

(for Tony)

Smoke means the way you looked the last time I ever saw you,
bare-chested above the Bay's ragged thunder, back pressed
against the scuffed bridge rail, scars so bright it seemed you
were already burning. Smoke means a rabbit might flee or set
itself in stone, means white semaphores of deer tails, cicadas
buried beneath root and soil waiting out the lightless years
before their single season of song. Smoke means embers adrift
in the shifting breeze, means a far-off fountain that gabbles its
wet canticle of before we were born. Smoke means the right
words will always fall stillborn. Where there's smoke,
something's vanished. Where there's smoke, I'll always see
you stepping through the dew grass that late-October morning
while our hemisphere tilted toward a longer dark. Then
gasoline. Then lighter. Then you in your shirt of flames.

The Agnostic's Prayer

O, you about whom much is said,
but none for certain,

are you the glint of evening copper
that sets the river's face aflame,
or the smoke-grey shadows that lengthen
across the backlit transept
of my father's riddled lungs?

Is it your voice I hear in the indigo
throat of the bunting,
or do you speak in tongues of flame
that turn crop fields to cinder?

Do you incense autumn
wind with the must of grapes
plucked from the vine,
or is your breath the roil of earth
and mud that flattens cities
when the levees finally crumble?

Do I taste you in the gold
of honeysuckle sipped
from the style, or in the tang
of venom sucked warm
from the wound?

Is it your finger that breezes
the plane of my chest
when I step into summer's first
shirtless dusk,

or will the fury of your fists
one day pound my heart
to stillness?

O, you who may or may not be
all—or any—of the above,
I attend at this strange equator
that divides *if* from *is*,
I am from *I am*
not,
I seek from *I have found.*

The Better Part

High summer on South Bass Island,
        and we wanted nothing

of the drunken tourists who littered
        the boardwalk or stood belly to belly

at the long pool bars, cheap speakers pumping
        a beat ancient as tribal drums.

The Angelus bells beckoned no one
        save us to the cave-cool church

where we climbed to the choir loft,
        sweat-slick, dizzy with desire,

and you went to your knees, lips soft
        as river moss upon me, my eyes fixed

on the stained-glass altarpiece
        where a man stood, mild-eyed

as a calf, half-clothed in grave linens
        too immaculate for their late service,

the day's new light sifting through
        his ragged palms like hourglass sand

while the woman he loved fell before him,
        the chalice of her hands open,

her touch rebuked, barely able, as he was,
        to keep his clotted feet on this earth,

aching, instead, to lift skyward.
        I wanted no part of that story

where flesh is exchanged for an eternity
        of tedious diminishment,

asked only for mortal communion,
        the sighs of old timber

as I pressed you to the pew,
        air redolent with candle smoke,

frankincense, and stale perfume.
        Even in the dizzy afterwards,

when the just-now-sated might cover
        their nakedness, turn their thoughts

toward the tattered hem of regret, I knew
        we'd chosen the better part,

even though it meant no stone
        would be thundered aside

to make clear our path to some afterlife
        that's nothing more than a shimmering

myth, in the same way a bass,
        having gained a chance reprieve

from the angler's hook, might return
        to its circling school to tell a tale

that begins in media res . . .
        the moment something unseen

snatched it from the lake's cerulean
        gravity into jubilant flight,

though it has no means to grasp
        the story's intended conclusion,

which was the ruin of air.

Each Thing That Has Been Taken

(Winchester Mansion, San Jose, California)

The dead do not care if their clothes catch and shred
on ribs of cypress hedge that guard the widow's
six-acre mansion. What need is there for cover
when they move, resplendent in their own raw gore,
across the scalped lawn in its shroud of starlight?

They stumble or crawl past the Serpent Fountain,
the bronze insult of Chief Little Fawn grasping
his impotent bow, reopen their wounds against the rough
skin of redwood shingles as they scale four scalloped stories
to the roof of this puzzle home, claw down the throats
of its seventeen brick chimneys.

The dead are hell-bent on taking back each thing
that has been taken . . . each missing limb whose absence
echoes in the faces of two hundred Victorian mirrors,
each shattered harp of rib and gristled spleen, each *this*
or *that* blown off or blown open by a Model 1873.

They have taken a vow to take their time, a blood toast
raised by each in turn to a slow descent into madness
for the one whose fortune was built on swift lever action,
whose ceaseless hours of hammer-fall sum up
her childish scheme of confusion or conciliation.

The dead have learned to savor the meanwhile,
to take the measure of incremental decline.
There is time enough to navigate the corridors and
twisted switchbacks, count to thirteen at each spindle and
webbed window, riffle through scrawled séance notes

kept by a withered hand. Time for each to squeeze
the old woman's sluggish heart as she rocks in her satin
bed, to keep her alive one more night and one more
night, until the last muzzle flash has been swallowed by
starless black. Until the last cursed bullet has been named.

Anorexia Mirabilis: Mary Magdalene de' Pazzi

In the lower choir where my sisters kneel
on rough wood, restless, black-beaded,

lost in reveries of glowing oven stones,
the coarse seed bread and churned butter

that will soon break the long hours of their fast,
I wait on nothing but you, Lord, unsteady as I am,

slow-pulsed and languorous beneath the weight
of my patched wool mantle. Still young,

monthly blood halted like all hope
of the damned, I am mother solely to desire

ravenous as a coliseum beast, and I will rise
only when the gold-throated bells have beckoned

You and I brush my lips against the priest's
warm fingers, swallow You who deigns enter me

white as a winding sheet before its terrible commission.
Like plaited thorns pressed to my crown, You stagger

me where this white wimple bends its nimbus
arc. You have inscribed the reliquary

of my heart with a secret to be read only when
I am laid open on the surgeon's table.

The Word Was Made Flesh and dwelt within me.
O, Love who descends in a garland of embers,

robes spilling off bloodied shoulders, I am
damp as a new bride who beholds the smooth

cursive that arrows from your waist to the rag
they hung above your sex for the sake of modesty.

Unworthy though I am, a virgin with a harlot's name,
I beseech You not for death but agony, not light

but doubt's brute refuge. Render me desolate
and hollow as an empty nave. Countenance

the cloister cupboards demon-gaped to illumine
glittering jars of late-summer preserves.

Conjure a years-long ache in my belly,
wolf sister to the bone whip that flays me.

No matter this starved-drunk equilibrium,
yellowed vellum of my skin, these bones

gone brittle as pendant ice, I remain
renunciate for Your name's sake, consent

to nothing but the unleavened moon
that conceals Your broken glory.

O Lord, I beg You, shatter me
with promises of the feast that is to come.

Dirge

I have seen monks burning
in their saffron robes for days,
coaxing sand from flutes
of silver while they bend
over floors or low tables
smooth as their solemn faces.
Like earth before it opens,
I have heard them hum,
tap kaleidoscopes of sand into
scintillant galaxies I long to fix
in their mad spinning,
though the monks will finish,
rise, circle that intricate perfection
with brushes to ghost the world
into glittering ruins
they'll sweep into glass vessels,
carry back to the sand's restless
maker, all the while
that thrum still thrumming
their throats as if to say, *Return
to the river, to the sea*—
the same wordless mantra
I caged inside my lungs
as I watched my father gather
his last throatful of breath,
then let it go the way
a soft-mouthed retriever
will drop a fallen hatchling,
unharmed, at his master's feet,
a leaving so gentle I couldn't

be certain he'd gone until twilight
swallowed the horizon,
a lightlessness that found its level
on either side of the hospital window
before I opened my fists
and found I had nothing to hold
on to but his feet going cold.
And my heart, my heart,
the fierce insistence of its dirge:
You have chased the wind
all of your days. Your hands
have always been empty.

Pietà

Matthew Shepard

(1 December 1976–12 October 1998)

Whether stony hill or barren field,
men will always tear at the mildest
among them, bone flail to flesh,
pistol to skull, wrists affixed with nails
or tied to rough-sawn timber—
so let mercy fall with its softer touch,
however late in this chill season,
a descent from crossbeam or buck-rail
into the arms of a mother
who's come full circle—
her boy still as sleep against her thighs.

Spontaneous Human Combustion

Fire's not a language of love,
        its legioned tongues not tidy as the heart
of Christ, which tells its lie of ravishing light
        that burns without singe or cinder.

Fire's a beast we love when it's caged,
        a warm flush beneath flesh, a secret
slight as the first spark of rage before it fans
        white-hot from the barrel of an oiled gun.

One minute an old woman settles into
        her worn leather chair, the next she's ash
and smolder, only a slippered foot
        as testament to her inexplicable combustion.

One minute a young man stalks the polished halls
        of his middle school, the next only muzzle flash
and scatter, the sprawled ghosts of sons and daughters
        quiet as what's been ossified by fire.

Longfellow's Beard

Here in this room she died; and soul more white
Never through martyrdom of fire was led
To its repose . . .
      "The Cross of Snow," Henry Wadsworth Longfellow

No wind that airless summer noon,
just a prayer for breeze as Fanny clipped
a few locks from Edith's sun-gold crown,
gathered what she meant to keep
for some day's *Remember when.*
No wind until after the match-strike,
a few red dribs of sealing wax fanned
like Hell's infernal downpour
against the gauze of my beloved's gown,
suddenly consumed to no more than a shift,
and she a lurch of burnt orange,
of howl, of stumble over the threshold
toward me, the rug I shawled around her
good for absolutely nothing. So, too,
the blunt twin torches of my flailing
hands before our last uncoupling
—two flames from one—then nothing
but the travesty of birdsong.
Eighteen years before I could transmute
memory into a cross
of snow, and all the while the secret kept
beneath this unkempt veneer—scars
like shades of the slender fingers
that once caressed, then scorched,
my countenance.

Turkey Buzzard Gospel

More infernal Venetian mask than flesh,
your visage haunts our sleepless hours,
dun beak like a scalpel that undoes crimson
mouthfuls of each creature we've broken
between bumper and macadam.
                      How blithely we move on,
rolling distance between ourselves and
our transgressions as you commence
the brute work of salvation, which declares
not all beauty derives from what's inviolate,
each tug a coarse lullaby, a paradox
that charms ruin into rising
through the corridors of your hollow bones,
while you, indifferent to our derision, bend
to preach your gospel of terrible mercy
that transmutes the awkward weight of what was
earthbound into the exaltation of flight.

Luna Moth

You will know two kinds of hunger,
the first, a smaller sadness—
a reciprocal thing that bends
the stave of your long, green days
toward splayed leaves of sweetgum,
fronds of walnut and smooth sumac
that will invoke, after long weeks
of exhortation, your exquisite
metamorphosis.

This is the hunger that drives you
to feed without ceasing,
not *as if* you cannot get enough
but simply *because*—
the hunger that will make you spin
around each viridian segment
of yourself a silken winding sheet
so you become your own still shade
sealed within that artifice,
a single leaf from the tree
in whose branches you will sleep
until you wake
to a strange annunciation
that splits along the hardened seam
of your solitude, calls you back
into a world of night,
your mouth not sealed but
disappeared, like the brief arc
of a falling star.

What's left will be
the lot of every hungry ghost,
a second hunger
that will exchange your sawtooth
mandible for seafoam wings
whose blind eyes face the stolen
light of your namesake moon,
while you drift, insomniac
with desire, through the seven
dwindling nights that are your destiny.

Here in this churchyard where you've kept watch

above the faithful these last two hundred years,
        the elements have conspired to erase you,

sharp pikes of your thorn-crown blunted by time
        and acid rain, nail heads that once pinned wrists,

crossed ankles, lost to winter's tug and pull
        on the thermometer's mercury

Even the rough wound in your side has been smoothed
        by caresses of widows who stood on tiptoe to beg

their husband's salvation, and by wind
        that, tonight, arrives beneath plumed Saharan dust

clouds borne six-thousand miles over Atlantic waves
        and great steel tankers, over legions of small towns

with their weathered bells and clapboard steeples—
        this wind that lends breath to the slow obliteration

of your agony, keeps company with you
        as with the dead who molder here beneath

wizened leaves and nodding hoods of snowdrops.
        O, savior broken for a cause I no longer believe in,

I pity you. I've lost my taste for your tortured
        extravagance. It is enough for me to know

stone is rolled to sand, sand is raised from crescent
     dunes, transmuted to this ephemeral light.

In the end, it will be beauty that saves me.

Miserere for George Floyd

(14 October 1973–25 May 2020)

Mercy for the boy behind the counter
      who accepts the blue-tinged twenty

      for the fingers that dial
      this unwarranted destiny

Mercy for the cop
      who would not kneel
      in solidarity
      now bending his knee
      to choke back breath

Mercy for the nine minutes
      it takes to crush the neck
      of a Black man

      for the dying man himself
      whose last words are a prayer
      to the one who brought him
      into this life

Mercy for her
      already two years dead
      unable to cradle her boy
      or kiss his cheek pressed
      to a street still warm
      with sunlight's waning

Mercy for neon's indifferent buzz
      for spring's gloaming
      that casts the day's last
      light without favor
      as if there's truth
      in the myth of equity
      as if it falls to each
      in equal measure

Cor Cordium

After Percy Shelley's death by drowning in 1822, his heart, plucked from the cremation pyre, was given to his wife, Mary. She kept this relic with her until her death nearly 30 years later.

How like him
      to choose fire
to forge a talisman
      out of the turquoise
waves that took him,
      to grant one final gift
whose song
      you'd only heard before
in the tristesse
      after passion,
your head above his heart
      and eased,
as if by an ocean's pulse
      held captive
in a polished shell.

Cor cordium,
      your dearest company,
the blessing and sure weight
      you'd carry
with the nonchalance
      of any indwelt thing,
silk-wrapped
      in a pocket,
or the spent star
      in your bureau drawer;

a hymn that sang itself
          against your ear
all those empty-bedded nights
          you held it close
as a conch shell lifted from sand.

Mary, what could it be
          you hoped for
those thirty years you listened
          to that heart song—
was it some grim assurance
          of eternity,
or just an aide-mémoire
          that to live even once
is its own best luck?

Between Oneself and the World

(after Bruegel the Elder's The Misanthrope)

Om dat de werelt is soe ongetru
Daer om gha ic in den ru

("Because the world is perfidious,
I am going into mourning")

There is the gold of coins
hard-won and warm
in a leather purse
strung to a bitter man's waist,
cut loose now
like a vestigial heart or
the plundered reliquary
of his youth.

There is the gold of morning
fields flecked with sheep
watched over by a man
who revels in the coarse music
of ruminant mouths
grazing incensed clover,
the sky-flung, metallic hum
of flies lifting
from each shivered coat.

Between oneself and the world
is simply the world
in all its shattered radiance.
The heart insists despite.

Spring Peeper Gospel

The hellebores are yesterday's
news to the jonquils who nod
their shirred bonnets
in time with the breeze. Here,
winter's grey palette dissolves
into vernal pools, conjures
tattered legions from mud
crypts, shield bark, leaf rot,
their primal chorus spilling
down verdant corridors.
I know too well the hunger
which gives rise to their song,
a parable that riddles eternity.
It is enough to know
this world will go on without me.

Nocturne for the Apocalypse

As if it was just another twilight,
no different from the last or yet-to-come,
we drew the blinds against each vanishing
as streetlights snapped on like charms
against erasures that moved like a draught of
hemlock over the tongue, numbing us
from the toes up, so slowly it was nothing
to pretend we didn't even recognize
the sigils of our ruin: summers unsung
by the canticles of honeybees, rainforests
stripped of their resplendent canopies,
the ragged ghosts of plunder
who rode the dusky tails of that receding light.

In those last days, night engulfed our cities
like the wings of a great swan
who scissored the moon in two,
another portent for which we claimed no cipher;
so too, the rain-blurred newsprint
that described another shooter run amok,
another glacier warmed to rivers that crested
above our bridge's white flood lines.

And all the while another republic fell
to anarchy, another Black man was choked
breathless for some fabricated crime,
another woman was buried shoulder-deep
in desert sand, her head caved in with stones.

And all the while the last ivory sickles were
hacked from the face of the last bull elephant,

and every work of human hands burned
with the imprimatur of the damned. Everywhere,
levies crumbled, coffins roiled out of earth and
drifted like rafts of refugees ocean-crashed by
waves called *Disappeared* and *Never Again*.

Emmett Till's Casket

In 2005, fifty years after his murder, Emmett Till's body was exhumed to repudiate rumors that someone else was buried in his grave. Having confirmed the body was his, it was placed in a new casket and reinterred. The original casket was restored and is now displayed in the National Museum of African American History and Culture in Washington, DC.

This is not a story that ends
        with a rolled stone,
cave walls singed by some ethereal flame
        that flashed before a brilliant
rising. This one's told in rust that gnawed
        the crook of each steel hinge,
in tarnished satin, in glass
        that kept its solitary watch
for fifty years above a face transformed
        by boot heels, bullets, barbed wire,
and the Tallahatchie's sunless bed.

This is not a story about a god-man
        with olive skin who wakes
in the hard place he was lain;
        this is the story of a Black child
who never woke
        to see fifteen, of his mother,
who beheld the interminable stillness
        of his face.

This is not a story about a virgin's
        dolorous heart pierced
by seven burnished arrows, her grief

　　　　tempered by the small wick
of hope she shelters against dying
　　　　　pre-Sabbath light.
This is the story of a mother denied
　　　　even the brief ministry
of cradling the meager weight
　　　　of her boy's ruined bones,
who lifted him, regardless,
　　　　in her refusal to turn—or let us turn—
from his terrible transfiguration.

The Martyrdom of Saint Serapion

(after Zurbarán)

As if from the spiced cool of an ancient tomb,
he appears to emerge from the tenebrous canvas.
No rumor of the jeweled loops of bowel gaped
behind the ashen scapular that mutely proclaims
the gospel he is martyred for,
rough serge streaming the threefold enigma
down to the confluence that, doubtless, flows
over his sandaled foot and from there on to
what is never-ending .
                  But for us, there is only paint
and the exquisite restraint of the artist's palette:
cinerary white for innocence reclaimed, incarnadine
and gold for the Mercedarian seal, a gloamy brown
for the leather cincture at the young man's waist,
his wounded brow brushed in shades of stormy
weather, ebony for the tousled hair that crowns
a head not yet half-sawn from the neck but presaged
by the way it seems to float unmoored amidst the waves
of his voluminous capuche.
                  Almost an afterthought,
inked on pale vellum, the name of the blessed is pinned
on the ghost tree to which he is affixed by ropes
that seem less manacle than coarse ovation,
unable to restrain such uncanny weightlessness,
as if, already, he is ascending.

Lament: Isis

Like ragged jaws of an oyster shell,
your coffin was pried open, flesh parsed

to fourteen glistening portions
flung wide across this fertile empire.

Desire conjured means for me to
gather that fearsome harvest,

shoulder blades bristling
with the sear of each feather's calamus.

Sharp-sighted, I flew between horizons,
gathered what had been cleaved

asunder, mended you like a maidservant
who turns her fish-bone needle to a torn

madder tunic, each stitch tucked
in an invisible hem. Beloved brother,

your rising would have been entire
had not your sex been consumed by

Nile fish and crocodiles. Now your new
reign must be over the dead

who have learned to live on nothing
more than memories of long-ago pleasure.

Madonna of Mariupol, Ukraine

*(after a photograph of an unnamed pregnant Ukrainian woman
being carried from a maternity hospital bombed by Russian invaders,
14 March 2022)*

Little mother-to-be,
      tawny hair pulled back
from the pallid moon
      of your visage,
eyes already fixed
      on something beyond
the picture's shelled periphery,
      how is it you came to be
hoisted into history by men
      who doubtless failed
to notice this frightful
      symphony of scarlets
—unlikely cheer
      of watermelon blanket,
deadly bloom between
      your thighs—
a ransom of blood
      and water spilled
from the lanced side
      of a dying king
or amnion's burst bubble
      being heaven's
favored currency.
      O god I no longer believe
in, tell me, how is it
      you declared this cold
banishment without need

of our petition? How is it
you still pronounce us
     unregenerate, make us
beg for an end
     to this, our exile?

Nocturne on the Danube Promenade

In Budapest, sixty sculpted pairs of iron shoes stand along the
Danube promenade, a testament to the thousands of Jews who were
executed there by Arrow Cross militiamen during the winter of 1944–
45.

Forgive us—
the crack-addicted hooker
who stumbles
along the promenade,
the lovers who think only
of themselves,
the corpulent street vendor
bellowing at passersby,
and me, who came empty-
handed to sit beside
these rusted shoes
that pool with votive light,
softened wax
taking on the contours
of absent flesh, the ghost
shape of your whispered
prayers in the white breath
of winter 1944 as you, guilty
of nothing,
man/woman/woman/child
linked hands
along the breakwall,
stepped from the familiar harbor
of your shoes,
the one thing of value
to the Arrow Cross guards,

who lowered their rifles
in the frost-singed dusk
after scarlet bloomed
mid-back and mid-back,
an infernal bouquet
dropped into the pallbearer
current as crows lifted,
sable-throated
along the embankment,
while spent rounds hissed
on frozen flagstone—
and the river,
knowing nothing
of its burden, carried on
toward the sea; the frigid
moon threw down its stolen
light, a wreath of bone
adrift on the unquiet surface.

Father Mychal Judge

(after the iconic photo of the priest's body being carried out of the World Trade Center's North Tower on 9/11)

Worse than a conflagration fed by kerosene,
than towers turned to their own sudden ruin,
worse than his already waxen hand,
its elegant fingers that seem poised for blessing,
is the square of flesh that must not have seen the sun
all that long summer, a glimpse of slender tibia
over which he'd pulled his plain cotton sock
when the morning was still ordinary,
still decipherable as a painted allegory
where ash gray stands for dreadful quietude,
as in marble made to bear an unbearable grief,
or the way men can emerge from a shroud of steel
and cinder carrying the slack weight of the fallen.
As if death is a burden they can help him carry.

Icarus

Never believe it was pride that dragged me
beneath the sea's cobalt meridian.

That morning, as my father bent under
the osier frame, drew tight
each supple strap of hide—
wrists to wingtips, shoulders to scapulae—
he breathed his stern mantra
into the conch of my ear:
Keep to the lower thermals—
too high, and the sun will strip
each quill from its tender socket.
Too low, and you will know
the dreadful weight of water.

How could he grasp
the way I longed for nothing
but light after the labyrinth's
ceaseless pitch,
to be no longer a boy but a star,
even in its radiant diminishing,
my view a glorious tumble
sky / sea / sky
then coins of spume
refracting dawn's hammered gold,
all desire extinguished
by salt and ultramarine?

Nocturne for My Final Breath

Bass clef of Cygnus's throat,
     Orion's brute cudgel,
and all you stars that burn
     without name or need
for anything more
     than your own terminal light,
what is it to exist
     without desire,
to be part of a distant myth,
     powerless to grant
or refuse a single thing
     but still wished upon
as you fall like tracers
     in some far-off war
I am ashamed to know
     so little of?
What is it to have no father
     who slouches across
the grainy fields of nightmare,
     the moon's sallow glow
turned the color of ruin
     by the copper that covers
his eyes, the staggered
     scuff of his shoes
tugging the grass
     like ruminant mouths
that tongue a language
     unfathomable
as the horizons you lantern?
     What is it to have no word
for the way I can't remember him

before his lungs
were shadowed like a Rorschach
    for the doomed?
Tell me,
    you who have never
drawn in the scent of sweetgrass,
    of a woman, or rain,
what prayer might I,
    who have no faith in any gods,
spend the last small coin
    of my breath on?
Only this:
    that my flesh might rise
from the flames
    that will consume it,
a constellation of cinders
    in the shape of a man
who turns the brief radiance
    of his face toward
your distant fires
    to wonder, once more,
at your beautiful indifference.

Acknowledgments

Thanks to editors of the following publications in which these poems first appeared, sometimes in different versions:

About Place: "Hellebore: Lenten Rose"

And Blue Will Rise over Yellow: An International Poetry Anthology for Ukraine: "Madonna of Mariupol, Ukraine" (as "Pietà: Madonna of Mariupol, Ukraine," 70–71. Edited by John Bradley. Austin, TX: Kallisto Gaia Press, 2023.

Asheville Poetry Review: "Altitude," "Nocturne for the Apocalypse"

Birmingham Poetry Review: "Anorexia Mirabilis: Catherine of Siena"

Briar Cliff Review: "Lazarus"

Catamaran: "After Wyeth," "Luna Moth," "Muse," "Rapture," "Spring Peeper Gospel"

Chagrin River Review: "Candlemas, 1933"

Comstock Review: "Lot's Wife"

Crosswinds Poetry: "Judas: Triptych," "Magdalene," "Pietà, 1998: Matthew Shepard," "The Whale," "Turkey Buzzard Gospel"

Cultural Weekly: "Where There's Smoke"

Ekphrastic Review: "Anorexia Mirabilis: Mary Magdalene de' Pazzi"

Fjords Review: "Each Thing That Has Been Taken"

Gettysburg Review: "A Kind of Benediction," "Here in this churchyard where you've kept watch . . . ," "To the Corpse of Alexander the Great"

Hayden's Ferry Review: "Blue"

Hole in the Head Review: "Apocrypha: The Ram Considers Abraham," "The Beloved Disciple," "Lucifer, Falling"

I-70 Review: "Faith," "Nocturne for an Unidentified Girl Found Murdered in a Field," "Rough Alchemy"

Indianapolis Review: "Evening Wind"

James Dickey Review: "Cor Cordium," "Death's Tailor," "Icarus," "Saint Fillan"

The Journal: "Filia Luminis"

Lake Effect: "Afterward: Magdalene," "Pietà: Father Mychal Judge"

Lily Poetry Review: "Still," "Terracotta Army"

Main Street Rag: "Nocturne on the Danube Promenade"

The Memory Palace: Ekphrastic Flash Fiction and Prose Poetry: "Longfellow's Beard," 125. Edited by Lorette C. Luzajic and Clare MacQueen. Toronto: Ekphrastic Editions, 2024.

The Night Heron Barks: "Daphne, Again," "What Light Is Given"

North American Review: "Dead Hummingbird"

Oberon: "The Martyrdom of Saint Serapion"

Palette Poetry: "Dirge"

Pedestal Magazine: "Nesyamun"

Pietà: "Benediction: Whale Fall," "Daphne, Again," "Dirge," "Each Thing That Has Been Taken," "Emmett Till's Casket," "Here in this churchyard where you've kept watch . . . ," "Lazarus' Wife," "Luna Moth," "Madonna of Mariupol, Ukraine," "Nocturne for My Final Breath," "Nocturne on the Danube Promenade," "Pieta, 1988: Matthew Shepard," " Pietà, 2001: Father Mychal Judge," "Spontaneous Human Combustion," "Thích Quảng Đức," "Topsy," and "Where There's Smoke." Edited by Richard Kraiwec. Durham, NC: Jacar Press, 2023.

Plume: "Sarah Bernhardt's Coffin"

The Power of the Feminine I: Poems from the Feminine Perspective: "Lament: Isis" (as "Isis and Osiris"), 218. Edited by Christal Ann Rice Cooper and Donna Biffar. ThreshPress Midwest, 2024.

Raven's Perch: "Between Oneself and the World," "Miserere for George Floyd"

River Heron Review: "Fiat to Autumn," "Saint Giles's Doe"

Rust + Moth: "Benediction: Whale Fall," "Upon Being Buried with My Twin"

South Florida Poetry Journal: "Thích Quảng Đức"

Taos Journal of Poetry: "Nocturne for My Final Breath," "The Forest"

Terrain: "The Griffon Vulture's Prayer"

32 Poems: "The Agnostic's Prayer"

Valparaiso Poetry Review: "For a Couple Who Died Two Days Apart"

"The Griffon Vulture's Prayer" was selected as a finalist in the 2023 Terrain.org Poetry Contest; "Lot's Wife" won second place, 2020 Muriel Craft Bailey Poetry Contest, selected by Patricia Smith; and *Pietà* won the 2023 Jacar Chapbook Competition, judged by Saddiq Dzukogi.

This book is dedicated to Julie Candela. Death cannot diminish my fondness for you, or my appreciation for your ability to grasp my work in ways beyond what others saw. I will miss your brilliance and unique perspectives on... everything, and I will never forget the four words you repeated to me many times over the course of our final conversations— *I am not afraid.*

I'm endlessly grateful to William Wright and Lise Goett, two incredibly talented poets who assisted me in shaping this manuscript into a cohesive whole. This book would not exist without your skillful guidance and encouragement.

Thanks to Roger Weingarten for believing in me and in these poems, as well as for your editorial advice and contribution in creating the cover art. The hours we spent on the phone discussing this manuscript were alternately instructive and amusing (with a dash of difficulty for good measure). You never pushed me to make any change I didn't believe in, and I know *Dark Octaves* would not be as strong as I trust it is without your generous assistance.

A special shout-out to Mary Barbara Moore, accomplished poet and dear friend, who bears the brunt of all my poetic and personal insecurities with love and grace. Your directness in calling out weaknesses in my poems is appreciated more than you know and has, I might add, saved me from public humiliation on more than a few occasions. But you also offer thoughts and suggestions on my more successful work, something that is both meaningful and advantageous. You've helped me grow as a poet and person, for which I am most grateful.

Another special shout-out to my friend, Rosa Lane, an all-around amazing human being and poet extraordinaire. Our meeting at Malaprop's Bookstore in Asheville, NC, was such a gift. Thanks for reading this manuscript so attentively and gracing it with your generous endorsement.

Thanks, too, to Nickole Brown, whose friendship has been a treasure I've cherished longer than any other such "poetic" relationship I've been fortunate enough to enjoy in this life. And to Marsha Huffman. I would have missed so much joy and laughter, as well as deep conversation, had you not taken the chance to ask that question all those years ago.

And, finally, to Lynne Knight, one of my newest (and best!) poet friends. We owe our meeting to Luke Johnson's generous invitation for us to read at his book launch for *Quiver* in November 2023, and we haven't looked back since. You are a treasure to me.

I also gratefully acknowledge Steph Forstner for the gift of support which, among other things, came in the form of several books wherein I first learned about some of the topics covered in this collection.

Gratitude to my dear friends whose comments and encouragement on early versions of these poems was indispensable: Julie Candela, Carrie Euype, Dan Lenk, Betty "Lou" O'Brien, and Zack Rogow. I hope you know how sincerely I value your thoughts, love, and encouragement. You inspire me to reach higher.

I'd be remiss if I didn't mention Carolyn Brown whose copyediting skills are the most impressive I've ever encountered. Your attention to detail is unmatched in my experience. This book is the beneficiary of your expertise and that means so much to me.

My gratitude extends to all the poets, writers, photographers, artists, and musicians whose work stirs me in ways I find mysterious and beautiful.

I am also indebted to the editors of publications in which these poems first appeared, as well as those who gave my work serious consideration, even if the ultimate answer was "no." The literary world would be nowhere without your tireless dedication.

Finally, and most important, my heartfelt thanks and love to my twin sister, Gerrie, who has stood by me with unfailing love and support through all my life's octaves, however bright or dark. You are my luckiest star!

About the Author

Frank Paino holds a BA in English from Baldwin Wallace University and an MFA in Creative Writing from the Vermont College of Fine Arts. Following graduation, he eschewed a teaching career in favor of a non-academic position at a university where he continues to work to this day.

He has received a number of awards for his work, including a 2016 Individual Excellence Award from The Ohio Arts Council, a Pushcart Prize and The Cleveland Arts Prize in Literature.

Other titles by Frank Paino:

Pietà Jacar Press
Obscura Orison Books
Out of Eden Cleveland State University Press
The Rapture of Matter Cleveland State University Press